The T

Knights

The Catholic Church's Most Powerful Warriors

Conrad Bauer

ISBN: 978-1723905827

Printed in the United States

MAPLEWOOD
– PUBLISHING –

Contents

Who Were the Teutonic Knights?

The Teutonic Knights were forged in the thick of battle, at the height of the Crusades in 1190 AD. But they weren't created to wield the sword—their first commission was to take care of the sick and the injured. Formed in the city of Acre, in what is now Israel, in the immediate aftermath of the fall of Jerusalem, the Teutonic Knights initially established field hospitals to aid the burgeoning number of wounded soldiers passing through this great way station of the Holy Land.

Jerusalem had been captured by the Crusaders scarcely 100 years before after Pope Urban II ordered knights from all over Europe to reclaim the city for Christ in 1095 AD. This First Crusade was quite successful; the Islamic defenders of the Holy Land were caught completely off guard by the alien invaders who suddenly stormed across the horizon with their strange metallic armor glinting in the desert sun. But a century later—after an ill-fated Second Crusade—everything had changed. A charismatic new Muslim leader named Saladin had managed to take back a large portion of what he believed to be Islamic real estate. Now on the defensive, the Crusaders had been forced to move the capital of their Kingdom of Jerusalem to the port city of Acre on the northeast coast of Israel.

And so it was that a Third Crusade was launched to regain the lost land. The German contingent was led by the Holy Roman Emperor Frederick Barbarossa—right up until he fell into a river in Armenia and drowned. This freak accident sent shock waves throughout the entire Crusader army, and with the loss of their Emperor, most of the German troops simply turned around and went home. The remaining Crusaders were mostly Britons and Frenchmen who found themselves woefully unprepared for the rigors of the Middle East.

Many of these men contracted illnesses related to the heat, contaminated water, and the like, and soon enough disease was running rampant through the Crusader camp. The Knights Hospitaller, established shortly after the First Crusade, were already managing a number of hospitals for the sick and dying, but it soon became clear that more was needed. A new monastic order called the Order of the Hospital of St. Mary was therefore created, and it was this group that would later become known as the Teutonic Knights.

Coming to the fold later than the Templars and the Hospitallers, the Teutons were somewhat like the little brother who has to fight for the remaining scraps at the table. Still, the Teutonic Knights of Acre ended up in control of the port of that famous sea city, becoming quite literally the gatekeepers of the Holy Land—and the tolls they collected turned out to be extremely profitable for the Order.

But their tenure in Acre was not to last. As the Islamic armies continued to roll back Crusader gains in the Middle East, seizing Jerusalem and much of the surrounding territory, the Teutonic Knights would soon have to outsource their talents for a variety of endeavors. Leaving their first estate and vocation behind, they would become free agents, spending the next few centuries chasing pagans, infidels, and heretics wherever they could find them.

Seeking Higher Ground

In 1210, the Teutonic Knights elected the man who was arguably their greatest leader of all time: Grand Master Hermann von Salza. A man of pure ambition, a real mover and shaker, Salza was a true medieval mogul. He was always promoting his Teutonic brand, and he was always on the lookout for the next big project for the Order. Furthermore, he had all the right connections to make sure that the Teutonic Knights always had the resources they needed to succeed. Grand Master Salza's most finely honed martial art was his ability to convince the wealthy men and institutions of his era to put their money and their moral authority behind the causes he presented to them.

Early evidence of this diplomatic skill came in 1211 when Salza secured a new home base for the Teutons by acceding to the entreaties of King Andrew II of Hungary that they set up shop in nearby Transylvania—the future stomping grounds of Vlad the Impaler (Dracula). In the centuries to come, Hungary would constantly be imperiled by its close proximity to the powerful Ottoman Empire. But at this point in time, King Andrew believed that he could bank on the Teutonic Knights to hold back the lesser threats posed by disorder in the wild borderlands. In exchange for their services, Andrew promised the Knights land and special immunities from taxes, which allowed them to bring settlers to the frontier without having to pay any indemnities to the Hungarian Crown. The partnership seemed quite successful at first. The Knights moved in, built fortresses, brought settlers, kept the peace, and soon felt confident enough to embark on their first major military engagement under Salza.

This was the Fifth Crusade, which came on the heels of the disastrous Fourth Crusade wherein Christian Crusaders had sacked Christian Constantinople without (for the most part) even reaching the Holy Land. The Fifth Crusade was the Vatican's effort to right the course of the Crusader ship by taking the fight back to the Islamic world with an invasion of Egypt. The plan was to use Egypt as a backdoor into Israel to reclaim lost territory.

In June of 1218, a combined force of Hospitallers, Templars, and yes, Teutonic Knights landed at the Egyptian coastal town of Damietta. The going was tough from the beginning, and the Templar Grand Master actually died shortly after going ashore. Despite this loss, the Crusaders' combined forces duly laid siege to Damietta and subdued it in fairly short order. Witnesses to the battle were particularly impressed by the manner in which the Crusaders rapidly overcame obstacles of the terrain. They used mobile pontoons to traverse a variety of landscapes, crossing crocodile-infested swamps with relative ease. It was obvious that the various orders had done their homework, and with the help of veteran Crusaders already familiar with the rigors of the Middle East, they were able to overcome daunting odds.

So impressive was their victory that the Sultan of Egypt—Al-Kamil, the brother of the mighty Muslim warrior Saladin—quickly offered the Crusaders a grand bargain. He proposed that he would hand over Jerusalem in exchange for the captured city of Damietta. Some of the Crusaders—the Teutonic Knights among them—were ready to accept this offer and go back to their faraway homes in Europe as victors. But it wasn't to be.

The acting religious leader of the Crusade, Cardinal Pelagius— who had full papal authority to make or break treaties as he saw fit—flatly refused Sultan Al-Kamil's overtures. Cardinal Pelagius apparently believed that with reinforcements from the Holy Roman Empire they would soon be able to take Cairo and then march on to Jerusalem on their own. But these anticipated reinforcements never left Europe, and the coalition of crusading knights was left to their own devices.

Nevertheless, Pelagius went ahead and commanded the group to move on toward Cairo to carry out the attack. The result was not good. The Crusaders were already overstretched in manpower and resources, and it didn't take much for Al-Kamil to outflank them. Soon an enormous Egyptian army was pursuing the knights up the Nile. With the Crusaders unable to turn around, the crafty Sultan literally opened the floodgates, causing the Nile to overflow and block their escape route.

Now, with the path ahead flooded and a massive contingent of Muslim warriors close behind, the Christian knights had only two choices—fight to the last man, or surrender to live another day. And while the Teutonic Knights would one day gain a fearsome reputation for fearless fighting in the face of death, that day was not yet come. Cooler heads prevailed, and the coalition opted for surrender.

Following this defeat, the Teutonic Knights spent several years regrouping in Europe under the direction of Grand Master Salza. The rebuilding effort was successful—too successful, in fact. In 1225, the Hungarian King Andrew II suddenly decided to kick his erstwhile champions out of Transylvania. The King, alarmed at the power base the Teutons were developing just across his border, had apparently decided that he would be better off facing a few raiding nomads than having a mighty military order perpetually camped out in his backyard.

The evicted Knights were once again looking for a new base of operations, and they found good demand for their services among other European leaders with problems on their barbarian-plagued borders. The countries on the frontiers of European Christendom were often raided by their pagan neighbors. The Old Prussians were particularly problematic in this regard. In 1218, for example, an Old Prussian horde had swooped down into the lands of Masovia (in what would today be northeast

Poland), wreaking absolute havoc and destroying some 300 churches. The Masovian leader, a certain Duke Conrad, was only able to get the plunderers to leave his land by paying a hefty bribe.

When news of these attacks reached the ears of the Pope, it gave him more than enough reason to unleash a new Crusade: the so-called Prussian Crusade. The main purpose of this little-known conflict was to push the pagan aggressors out of Christian territory, but of course, the additional objective was to convert as many of them as possible. Although the campaign was carried out under the orders of the papacy, operational matters were left to Duke Conrad.

The Duke officially enlisted the military services of the Teutonic Knights in 1226. In exchange for taking on his pagan enemies, Conrad promised them wide swaths of Chelmno Land, and the Knights—who were now "free-lancers" in the most original sense—seized upon this quest with all the zeal they could muster. At first, all was well—but it wouldn't be long before Conrad, like Andrew before him, would begin resent the Teutons' growing power.

Meanwhile, though, things were taking a decidedly strange turn for the members of the Order who had remained in the Crusader outpost of Acre. It all began with the arrival of their imperial patron, the Holy Roman Emperor Frederick II. Avidly discussed by historians as one of the most extraordinary characters of his age, Frederick was indeed highly unusual for his time. Ever since coming to power at the tender age of three, Frederick had been an incredibly inquisitive person. He was a polyglot, speaking German, Greek, Italian, French, Latin, and even Arabic with ease. This last enabled him to engage seamlessly with the Muslim world, and it is said that Frederick was in fact quite enamored with the Muslim culture of the Middle East—an admiration that did indeed set him apart from his contemporaries.

Frederick and a contingent of Imperial troops arrived at the gates of Acre on September 7, 1228. There was one problem, though: The Crusader city had just received word that Frederick had been excommunicated by the Pope. The reason given was Frederick's previous defiance of papal authority, including his failure to answer the call to Crusade. Of course, this does seem rather bizarre when you consider that the knights of the Fourth Crusade, who had boldly defied the Pope's instructions by sacking Constantinople and senselessly spilling the blood of the very Christians they were supposed to protect, had suffered no such penalty. Yet Frederick, who had simply failed to jump to the Pope's beck and call fast enough, was excommunicated outright. Clearly, there was more to the story, and most historians believe that the excommunication was simply the end result of a friction between Emperor and Pope that had been building for quite some time.

At any rate, the Templars and Hospitallers who held most of the power in Acre took the Pope's side and were now dead set against Emperor Frederick. The Teutonic Knights, who could not bring themselves to reject their fellow German and great benefactor, were the only ones who remained steadfast in his defense.

Unable to rally the support he needed to carry out the intended Crusade to recover Jerusalem by force, the wily Frederick leveraged his skills as a negotiator and his fluency in Arabic to craft a deal with Muslim leaders that granted him control of Jerusalem for a period of 10 years on the condition that Muslims would still have unrestricted access to the Temple Mount, where their holy shrines of Al-Aqsa Mosque and the Dome of the Rock were located. Considering that not a drop of blood had to be spilled to reach the agreement, this was a stunning achievement.

The Templars and Hospitallers were loath to acknowledge it, however, and their hostility bordered on open violence and talk of insurrection against Frederick. Only his imperial subjects, the Teutonic Knights, remained at his side, and thus when Fredrick was crowned as the new King of Jerusalem, it was the Grand Master of the Order, Hermann von Salza, who gave a speech in the Emperor's honor. Few others in the Crusader States wished to bestow such an honor upon the excommunicated Emperor, though, and on May Day of 1229, when Frederick set sail from the Port of Acre, the citizens of the town celebrated by throwing rotten vegetables and cowpats at his entourage.

With their own Holy Roman Emperor so sorely treated, the Teutonic Knights knew that it wouldn't be long before they would have to seek some higher ground of their own.

The High Price of a Prussian Peace

As tensions grew worse in the Holy Land, the Teutonic Knights in Europe found themselves engaged in a campaign against the pagan Old Prussians that would last some 50 years. The war was particularly brutal, even by the standards of the Crusades. It is said, for example, that upon capturing a Teutonic Knight, the Prussians would roast him alive "like a chestnut" inside the very armor that he wore. For their part, the Knights waged nothing short of a war of extermination, extending mercy only to those Prussians who agreed to be baptized.

Once the pagans were put down in a particular area—either by the sword or through forced conversion—the Teutons began to settle the newly conquered territory immediately. They recruited waves of immigrants from German lands, bringing with them an intelligentsia of skilled artisans, traders, and bankers. This was hardly what Duke Conrad had hoped for—he had conceived of the Prussian Crusade as a temporary measure to secure his borders and did not intend for the Teutonic Knights to settle down permanently. But he had little choice but to acquiesce as the Teutonic Knights conquered large tracts of pagan land and installed their new base of operations squarely on Masovia's eastern frontier.

The independent state that the Order formed became known as the Monastic State of the Teutonic Knights. This new nation was heavily fortified with castles and battlements all along its eastern border. But the Teutons weren't the first monastic order dedicated to keeping watch on the last pagan holdouts of Eastern Europe.

In the nearby nation of Livonia resided the remnants of a local group of Christian enforcers known as the Livonian Brothers of the Sword. This Catholic military order had been established in 1202 but utterly defeated in 1236 by the Lithuanian pagans that they had sought to tame. Some 50 to 60 Livonian Brothers were killed in their last battle, with their leader, Master Volkwin, among the casualties, and following this crushing blow the brotherhood—along with all its temporal holdings—was absorbed by the Teutonic Knights. Over the next few centuries, Livonia would become one of the Order's main strongholds.

It would also come to hold a very special place in their monastic heart of hearts. Someone had once decided to designate Livonia as St. Mary's Land, and since the Teutons had originated as the Hospital of St. Mary this particular patron saint had immense significance for the Order. Just as Palestine/Israel was believed to be the land of Christ, the Teutonic Knights began to view Livonia as the territory of Mother Mary on Earth. The Baltic is certainly a bit far removed from Bethlehem, but the Knights were still willing to push this notion forward—and they weren't alone.

This sentiment actually echoed what had already been declared at the Fourth Lateran Council in 1215. In regard to this region on the Christian frontier, one Bishop Albert had famously pleaded, "Holy Father, as you have not ceased to cherish the Holy Land of Jerusalem, the county of the Son, with your Holiness's care, so also you ought not abandon Livonia, the land of the Mother, which has hitherto been among the pagans and far from the cares of your consolation and is now desolate. For the Son loves his Mother and, as he would not care to lose his own land, so too, he would not care to endanger his mother's land."

However sincerely held, the concept also had immense strategic value as propaganda, encouraging the defense and settlement of what Western Europeans generally considered to be the backwater wilderness of their world. And the Teutonic Knights heartily endorsed this branding of Livonia as they built their new nation around it, no doubt reasoning that many Catholics would feel more welcome in a land spiritually claimed by the Sacred Madonna herself than they would on the wild frontier.

Soon after assuming control of Livonia, the Teutonic Knights began to conduct campaigns as far afield as Russia. Now, the Christian Russians might seem like rather odd enemies for Crusaders, but in the eyes of the Catholic—and expansionist—Teutons, their Orthodoxy made them a heretical sect and therefore fair game. However, their plan to force the Russians into the Catholic fold ultimately failed when they were pushed back by the Novgorod leader Alexander Nevsky in the dramatic 1242 engagement known as the Battle of the Ice.

In a tactic that has been repeated several times in Russian history, the invading Crusaders were lured into engaging the Russians on a frozen lake. The Teutonic Knights and their Livonian allies quickly rushed over the ice to do battle with their opponents, but their advance was soon checked by the formidable Russian front lines. After two hours of intermittent fighting, the heavily armored knights' biggest challenge was often just to keep from slipping on the ice. With his enemy discouraged and disoriented, Alexander then sent in the cavalry, ordering both the right and left flanks of his army to close in and threaten to surround the weary Teutons. Understanding the precariousness of their situation, the Crusaders began a frantic retreat. But in their haste, the ice began to crack, and to their horror, many of them went crashing through the surface of the frozen lake. The survivors watched helplessly as their comrades, shining suits of armor and all, sank down through the frigid water to perish at the bottom. After this resounding defeat, the Teutonic Knights would not return to Russia for another 100 years.

But it was in that same year of 1242 that the Order began to have trouble with the Pomeranian Duke Swantopolk II. For most of us today, probably the only thing that comes to mind when we hear "Pomeranian" is the cute little dog, but at one time such a nation did indeed exist. Medieval Pomerania was made up of parts of what is now northeastern Germany and northwestern Poland—and Swantopolk was conspiring with the freshly converted Prussians of the region to overthrow the Monastic State of the Teutonic Knights.

Interestingly, the Duke apparently didn't object to the Knights per se, but to the hangers-on who had come with them. It seems that the German settlers who had followed the Knights from the Holy Roman Empire were eating up all the trade in the region, and Duke Swantopolk was determined to put a stop to it. From the Teutonic perspective, though, the Order had done Polish noblemen such as Swantopolk a great service by ending the constant Old Prussian raids. The Knights, therefore, viewed the Duke's double cross with the utmost disgust and contempt.

His treachery also posed quite a serious danger. When the Knights had first arrived on the besieged Polish frontier, Swantopolk had been one of their staunchest allies. This meant that he was intimately acquainted with all of their strategies and tactics. He knew, for example, that the Knights always sought to fight on open, even terrain close to their fortress. He realized that this allowed them to maximize the advantage of their formations of heavily armored knights and bowmen, and he accordingly sought to disrupt this strategy by surprising the Knights with random assaults on their castles.

Many of the Teutonic fortresses were decimated in this fashion as repeated raids caught the denizens off guard and negated their superiority in arms with the overwhelming numbers of native Prussians. It is said that some 4,000 Germans lost their lives in these attacks. The Knights only managed to rebound with a ferocious assault at the heart of Pomerania in which they, in turn, destroyed the fortress of Sartowitz. However, intermittent fighting between the factions continued until Christmas Eve of 1247, when the Knights seized the largest remaining Pomeranian fortification and destroyed it, effectively breaking the back of the resistance.

By 1260, though, the Prussians rebelled against their Teutonic overlords once again. The leader of this uprising was a man named Henry Monte, and just like Duke Swantopolk some 20 years before, Monte knew the Teutonic Order inside and out. His knowledge, however, stemmed from the time he had spent with the Order as a prisoner of war in previous conflicts. So as you can see, Monte had both the means and the motive to use the Knights' own strategies against them. Prussian fighters were also much better equipped by this point, with armaments on par with those of the Teutonic Knights. They now had their own heavy armor and crossbows, as well as siege engines with which they were able to reduce many previously impregnable Teutonic castles.

For the next six years, the Prussians waged a winning war against the Teutonic Knights, taking out fortress after fortress, with the Teutonic capital of Konigsberg only saved by last-minute reinforcements from Livonia. The fighting petered out after that but did not end until the last Prussian resistance to Teutonic authority was finally stamped out in 1283. Peace had been bought but at an extraordinarily high price.

War Against Lithuania Begins

In 1291, the last Crusader foothold in the Holy Land, Acre, was lost to the Mamluk Sultanate. It was a valiant struggle that had the Templars, Hospitallers and Teutonic Knights fighting side by side, but they were vastly outnumbered and it was only a matter of time before they were completely overwhelmed. The few Teutonic Knights who escaped the siege found their way to Venice, and it was as they regrouped there that Holy Roman Emperor Frederick II gave them the assignment that would lead them to the high point of their history: He asked the Knights to wage a war of conversion against the people of Lithuania, Estonia, and any remaining pagans in Prussia, giving them his express permission to do anything and everything they could and to use all resources at their disposal from their base in Livonia.

While the Teutonic Knights were fighting the early skirmishes of this war, their fellow Crusader order, the Knights Templar, received a deadly blow—not from any outside foe, but from within the heart of Christian Europe. Although they had failed to hold on to the Crusader States of the Middle East, the Templars had amassed incredible wealth, and this had attracted the resentment of many of the European countries that now hosted them. Many European heads of state were in fact in debt to the order, which had been operating as a kind of pseudo-bank for many years, issuing loans to kings, queens, and emperors all over the continent.

One of these indebted potentates was King Philip IV of France. He owed a considerable sum to the Templars, and he also resented the armed encampment they had formed inside his kingdom. Not wishing to pay back his loans or play host to an independent paramilitary group, the French King decided to act against them. Working with the Pope, he was able to build up a heresy case against the Templars, and in October of 1307, on Friday the 13th, his troops stormed the Templar headquarters in a surprise raid and placed all whom they found within under arrest.

Those prisoners were immediately subjected to a brutal inquisition in which they were forced to confess to all of the charges that King Philip and the Pope had brought against them. These "confessions" ranged from sacrilegious rituals to sodomy to outright Satanism. Even though the Templar Grand Master later recanted his own confession and revealed that his fellow knights had all been tortured into making theirs, he and most of the rest of the leadership were quickly executed and the order was disbanded. All Templar property and wealth in Western Europe was then seized by the French Crown.

The Teutonic Knights studiously bore witness to these grave events and came to the conclusion that, in order for them to avoid the same fate, they needed to have a place to call their own. They couldn't rely on the courtesy of European kings—they needed nothing short of their own nation. This realization rallied the Teutons to their extraterritorial ambitions in Eastern Europe more than ever before. If they could carve themselves a big enough piece of Livonia, Lithuania, and Prussia, they knew that there would be no one to kick them out. With this in mind, they renewed hostilities against the pagans of Lithuania.

The Lithuanians well understood the threat they faced, and the Teutonic aggression soon cemented their disparate tribes closer together. By 1316 they had formed a veritable Lithuanian super-state under the rule of Grand Duke Gediminas. While not a whole lot is known about Gediminas, it can be confirmed that he was born to a Lithuanian nobleman named Pukuveras sometime in the 1270s. But it was his brother, Grand Duke Vytenis, from whom Gediminas received authority to rule over Lithuania—thereby establishing a dynasty that would last until 1572.

Gediminas' struggle against the Teutonic Knights began rather early in his reign with intermittent skirmishes with the Order as well as allied Germanic states. As hostilities heated up, Gediminas found an unlikely ally in the nomadic Tatars who had long been pillaging and rampaging through Eastern Europe. The Tatars were also allied with the Mongolian juggernaut founded by Genghis Khan, which had subdued much of Eastern Russia by this time. The Duke and his allies put up a strong resistance to the Teutonic Knights, and Lithuania thrived under his guidance. He expanded the borders of his nation all the way to the mouth of the Niemen River, where an outpost of Teutonic Knights looked on.

Then, in July of 1320, the Order launched a massive attack that drove far inside Lithuania, pushing Gediminas' army back and taking numerous captives along the way. But the Knights would not leave this engagement unscathed. As they attempted to return to their base in the Monastic State, they were waylaid in the wild Samogitian region by a small band of guerrilla fighters who managed to kill a total of 29 Knights.

It was not a heavy loss, but for a finite order such as the Teutonic Knights, in which keeping sufficient levels of manpower was always an issue, every single Knight lost was one too many. In late 1322, the Teutonic Knights recruited a number of foreign fighters to supplement their ranks and aid them in their conquest of Lithuania. The cadre included troops from Bohemia, Swabia, Silesia, and the Rhineland. This motley crew of mercenaries totaled around 20,000 warriors—truly an impressive auxiliary force to augment the dwindling band of true Knights.

This coalition was then unleashed in the same Samogitian region where the Knights had been ambushed two years before. The attack decimated several villages and fortifications, sending a clear message to the Grand Duke of Lithuania that the Teutonic Knights were ready to reassert their dominance. But Gediminas had a message of his own to deliver. Amassing a huge army, he sent it crashing into the Teutonic territory of northern Livonia, rampaging through the region before absconding with some 5,000 captives.

Gediminas was a great military strategist, and he was also an adept politician and statesmen. He proved as much in late 1322, when even while fighting the Teutonic Knights on the battlefield, he began direct negotiations with the Vatican to get them off his back. In a bid to neutralize the Teutonic threat, he asked to be baptized into the Catholic faith and opened the door to the possibility of Christian missionaries being sent to his country. The Pope was quite happy to hear such news, but the Teutonic Knights weren't quite so ready to accept their old Lithuanian nemesis as their new Christian brother.

This became especially obvious in February of 1336 when a combined force of 6,000 French, German, and Austrian soldiers led by the Teutonic Knights launched an invasion deep into the heart of Lithuania. Here they assaulted the Pilenai hill fort, which was a major defensive installation for the Lithuanian military. Along with Lithuanian warriors, however, this fortress also contained a large group of unarmed citizens who had sought semi-permanent refuge in the citadel for protection from the constant Teutonic raids against their villages.

Pilenai was overseen by none other than Grand Duke Gediminas' brother Margiris. The defenders were greatly outnumbered, and when the compound's walls began to crumble, a desperate decision was made. It was determined that rather than surrender, they would burn all of their valuables, kill their women and children, and then kill themselves and each other. Some contend that this was the largest mass suicide in history, with over 5,000 people tragically choosing to take their own lives.

When the Crusaders finally breached the walls, expecting to loot and take captives, they found nothing but charred corpses and burnt supplies. To be sure, the Teutonic Knights and their comrades had won the battle, but once again, they had very little to show for it. Whether, at this point in their history, any individual members of the Order felt that they were losing their way is very hard to know. But the Teutonic Order as a whole was determined to march on nonetheless, believing that whichever way the winds of fate blew, they would be guided by divine providence.

The Polish/Lithuanian Union

Although Gediminas made several overtures to the Catholic Church and at one point even asked to be baptized, most accounts state that the Grand Duke of Lithuania remained a pagan ruler of a still mostly pagan nation until the day he died. In fact, during his elaborate funeral in 1341, he was apparently given full pagan rites—including several human sacrifices in which his own servants were burned alive on his funeral pyre. So in all probability, his attempts at diplomacy with the Vatican were just that—diplomacy. Gediminas' expressed interest in the Christian faith was most likely merely a strategy to relieve the constant pressure of Teutonic attacks upon Lithuania.

In any event, the Teutonic Knights upped the pressure once again just a few years after his death. On February 2, 1348, they delivered a devastating defeat to Gediminas' son, Grand Duke Algirdas. Despite being considerably outnumbered, the Knights were able to destroy the fortress of Veliuona, significantly rolling back recent Lithuanian gains. This stunning blow led many Lithuanian leaders to once again discuss conversion to Christianity—if once again for no other reason than to get the Teutonic Knights off their backs.

For a moment it seemed that all of the violence and bloodshed was finally going to fulfill the Teutonic Knights' prime directive of converting the pagans. But some hardline adherents of the old faith held on, clinging to their guns and their religion, and in the end, Lithuania did not become an official part of the Christian fold until 1387.

Its then Grand Duke, Jogaila, had been baptized into the faith the year before simultaneously with his marriage to the Polish Queen Jadwiga, and this monumental union would unite Poland and Lithuania for the next few centuries. After Jogaila took over as King of Poland, his cousin Vytautas became the new Grand Duke of Lithuania, assuming control of all military matters in 1392. With Lithuanians on the thrones of both Poland and Lithuania, the stage was set for a titanic war between this Polish/Lithuanian union and the Teutonic Knights.

It didn't take much to set off the hostilities; the spark that lit this conflagration was a small uprising of Prussians in the Monastic State of the Teutonic Knights. It was discovered that Lithuania had backed this rebellion, and the Knights threatened to overrun Lithuania in revenge. Poland stood firm with its ally and declared that if the Teutons tried it, Poland would invade their Prussian holdings in reprisal. The current Grand Master of the Teutonic Order, Ulrich von Jungingen, issued an official proclamation of war against both Poland and Lithuania on August 6, 1409, setting history irrevocably into motion.

After getting off to a slow start, the long-awaited war broke out in earnest in the summer of 1410 in the vicinity of the villages Grunwald and Tannenberg, out on the open plains of Prussia. At first, the Teutons appeared to be waging a successful campaign. They stormed the castle in Dobrin, captured the Polish towns of Bobrowniki and Bydgoszcz, and raided many towns in between. Grand Master Jungingen initially followed the traditional Teutonic strategy of playing it safe, not rushing into battle, and consolidating gains with a slow advance.

But after he received word of the outrages that the Poles/Lithuanians and their Tatar allies were perpetrating on local villages and churches, his anger got the better of him and he decided to lead a surprise attack on the main enemy encampment. The only problem was—the attack wasn't much of a surprise. When Jungingen and his Teutonic Knights charged toward the town of Tannenberg, the enemy was expecting them.

Jungingen then made a second mistake by having his troops advance just far enough to dig defensive trenches. These were meant to hinder enemy cavalry charges. But oddly, wanting to make room for reinforcements that arrived on the scene, Jungingen ordered his men to withdraw shortly afterward. This hasty retreat turned the painstakingly dug trenches over to the enemy, making them a part of their own defenses. Now, in order to attack their foes, the Teutonic Knights would have to charge over these very pits. The men involved had essentially been digging their own graves.

From here, things quickly went from bad to even worse. The real trouble began when the Lithuanian army tricked the Teutons into thinking that they were attempting to retreat. A large group of

Lithuanian light cavalry rode off into the woods behind them, pretending to be withdrawing from the battlefield. Seeing the Lithuanians apparently making a run for it, a number of the Teutonic Knights gave chase. Unbeknownst to them, however, Polish troops were waiting on the sidelines to ambush them.

When Grand Master Jungingen saw what was happening he ordered his own contingent to form a tight wedge-shaped formation to charge directly at the Poles who had ensnared the group of Teutonic Knights. Trying to steal victory from defeat, he boldly aimed his men directly at the royal entourage, hoping to deliver a knockout blow by killing King Jogaila.

But just then Lithuanian reinforcements began to rush out of their hiding spots in the nearby forest, rapidly overwhelming the Teutonic Knights. Jungingen's charge failed, his group unable to get past the royal bodyguards who quickly rallied around their liege. Realizing his mistake, the Grand Master began screaming the order "Retreat! Retreat!" But it was too late. He and his unit were completely surrounded.

Jungingen and his group of knights were then cut to pieces by the Polish guards. It remains unclear exactly how Jungingen died, but there is one fanciful story that has been passed down which suggests that he actually perished in hand-to-hand combat with Jogaila himself. According to this legend, Jogaila and Jungingen charged at each other, and Jogaila, turning ever so slightly at the last minute, managed to brush Jungingen's lance harmlessly to the side while his own lance struck home right into Jungingen's neck. Jungingen then fell to the ground with Jogaila's lance still protruding from his throat, his body twitching and writhing in agony as he bled to death.

One thing, however, is certain: Jungingen did not survive the skirmish. And as soon as his Knights saw that their Grand

Master was dead, they panicked. Seeking to flee the battlefield, they turned what should have been a tactical retreat into a complete rout. Turning to run, the frontline Knights soon found themselves unable to move past all of the soldiers, horses and siege equipment of the rear guard. Pinned between their own troops and the enemy, these poor, pitiful souls had little choice but to attempt surrender or die fighting a hopelessly lost battle. The remaining ranks attempted to stave off the inevitable by positioning wagons tied together with metal chains as a makeshift barrier, but the emboldened enemy tore through these haphazard fortifications in rapid succession. The Polish/Lithuanian army soon overran the entire Crusader encampment, slaughtering everyone who remained.

The few Teutonic Knights who managed to make a clean break and ride off in the other direction were doggedly pursued all the way back to the Teutonic stronghold of Marienburg Castle. Here the enemy forces besieged the Knights for the next couple of months but were finally repelled when reinforcement from Livonia arrived on the scene. However, hostilities didn't officially end until the so-called Peace of Thorn was arranged in 1411. In the end, the Polish/Lithuanian union had proved to be too much for the Teutonic Knights to handle.

And some say that the Knights weren't very gracious losers. At least one local legend paints a picture of them venting their wrath on the Poles still under their dominion. According to chroniclers from the Polish city of Danzig (now known as Gdansk), shortly after the Teutonic Knights were defeated in the Battle of Tannenberg, they levied a hefty tax on the city's residents.

Danzig's Burgermeister, Konrad Lezkau, had the audacity to complain, and his succeeded protest succeeded—in bringing the wrath of his Teutonic overlords down on his own shoulders. Lezkau and three of his associates eventually met with the

Order's local leaders to ease tension, and at first, this effort appeared to have paid off. The authorities even invited their reconciled subjects to the feast they were hosting for the annual Palm Sunday celebration at their castle.

The men heartily accepted and made their way to the fortress on the appointed day. When they arrived at the gates they were oddly greeted by the court jester, who made the cryptic comment, "If only you knew what they were cooking—you might not come to eat!" One of the Poles caught the undercurrent of menace in these strange words and immediately made an excuse to leave. The other three, however, passed it off as a joke on the jester's part and continued on into the castle.

Before they could even take their seats at the banquet table, the Knights who greeted them made it clear that they weren't exactly guests of honor. Their hosts began interrogating them and subjecting them to vitriol of the worst kind, severely chastising them for daring to question the authority of their Teutonic masters. After several minutes of such abuse, the Knights brought forth Danzig's official hangman and told him to string up the dinner guests right then and there. The executioner, however, turned out to be a true professional who wouldn't work without a death warrant signed by a judge. For his unflagging commitment to the rule of law, the hangman was taken outside and flogged.

The frustrated Knights then took matters into their own hands and butchered the three dignitaries from Danzig forthwith. They took their broadswords and stabbed, cut, hacked, and chopped their dinner guests until they were reduced to mangled piles of flesh and blood strewn before the dining table.

Then came the cover-up as the Knights attempted to keep their atrocity hidden behind the thick walls of their castle. Soon, though, the men's wives began asking after them. Initially, the Knights told them that their husbands were simply in the middle of a prolonged discussion on the tax issue. The women didn't believe this explanation, but they still didn't suspect the awful truth; they thought that perhaps the men had been imprisoned inside the fortress.

Concerned for their husbands' welfare, they began bringing the castle guards foodstuffs to hand to their husbands. The murderous—and apparently hungry—Knights cruelly seized upon this gesture by pretending to pass on messages about what the men wanted their wives to bring them. This, of course, was actually what the gluttonous Knights wanted to eat, and as soon as they received these medieval care packages, they gobbled up the dead men's food themselves.

As the days dragged on, however, the wives' concern for their husbands grew more dire, the surviving Danzig officials began to question the whereabouts of their colleagues, and the Teutonic Knights grew weary of their game. In order to end it, they unceremoniously dumped the butchered bodies of the murdered men outside the castle walls as a crowd of citizens looked on. Despite the sobs of the newly widowed women ringing in their ears, the Polish authorities could do nothing but grimly bury the slain.

The jury is still out on how exaggerated this tale may have become over the years, but by many accounts, this capacity for extreme vindictive cruelty by some members of the Teutonic Order is not too far off the mark.

The Reformed Teutonic Knights

Even after the Peace of Thorn, the Teutonic Knights continued to skirmish intermittently with the Lithuanians and Poles. The 1422 Treaty of Lake Melno, which stipulated that the Order would cease its ongoing attempts to seize territory from the Grand Duchy of Lithuania, finally settled things with that nation, but Poland was another story. In 1431 Grand Master Paul von Rusdorf struck out against the Polish once again, starting the

Polish-Teutonic War. This struggle ended in 1435, following which the Monastic State enjoyed nearly two decades of peace.

Then, in 1454, a group of West Prussian noblemen calling themselves the Prussian Confederation decided to take on the Order in what would become known as the Thirteen Years' War. The Knights were forced to sell their territory of Neumark in 1455 to pay for the conflict, and by the end, they had lost another large chunk of their holdings. However, it was Prussia that bore the brunt of the fighting, and much of the nation was laid waste before the signing of the Second Peace of Thorn in 1466. This treaty granted West Prussia to Poland, finally giving the Poles access to the Baltic through the port city of Danzig. The Teutonic Knights were allowed to keep their holdings in East Prussia, but they were also required to pay homage to the King of Poland.

This was certainly a significant blow to the Order, and another great loss of territory loomed in the future. This one came not at the point of the sword, but at the baptismal font. To the astonishment of his colleagues, in 1525 the Knights' own Grand Master, Albert of Brandenburg, left Catholicism for the Protestant faith of Lutheranism. Nowadays, such a conversion from one Christian denomination to another wouldn't seem like a big deal to most people. But for Catholics of the early 16th century, it was nothing short of heresy, punishable by death—and all the more shocking when done by the head of a major monastic order.

Unbeknownst to the Vatican, Albert had become very good friends with Martin Luther—so good that when Pope Hadrian VI directed him to reform the Teutonic Order, it was this architect of the Protestant Reformation to whom he turned for advice. Needless to say, it was not advice of which the Pope would have approved. During a clandestine meeting on November 29, 1523, Martin Luther told the Grand Master to "throw aside the foolish and absurd rules of the Order, marry, and convert the religious state into a secular state, either a principality or a duchy."

Grand Master Albert was ready to leave the celibate life—and even the entire Monastic State of the Teutonic Knights—behind. And so, unlikely as it may seem, he took Luther's advice, renounced his vows, and married a Danish princess named Dorothea in 1526. He took the rest of Prussia with him when he went.

It is an aspect of history that is not much spoken of, but it turns out that there is a little more to the story than Albert's own dramatic conversion. Martin Luther had been actively seeking to win over the Teutonic Knights for many years. They were, after all, the major Catholic fighting force in the area, so it only made sense for the German monk to seek to bring them over to his side as a major disrupter to use against the Vatican. And Martin Luther was nothing short of prolific in his proselytizing for the Knights to join the Protestant Reformation. In one missive directed to the Teutons, for example, he authoritatively declared:

"Marvel not, dear Knights of the Teutonic Order, that I have made bold to address to you a special writing, and to advise you to give up your unchaste chastity and to marry. My intentions are altogether good. Besides, many sincere and intelligent men regard it as not merely helpful, but even necessary, to look to you to do this, because your order is indeed a unique order, differing from others most of all in that it was founded for the purpose of making war against the infidels. It must, therefore, wield the worldly sword and be a secular order at the same time that it is to be a spiritual order and make and keep the vows of chastity, poverty, and obedience like other monks. How that combination works, daily experience and reason teach us only too well. Besides, the knights are suspected and disliked because everyone knows how rare chastity is, and every man must be afraid for his wife and daughter. For they who are not married cannot be trusted very far since even they that are married must be constantly on their guard lest they fall, although among them there is more justification for hope and confidence. Among the unmarried, there is neither hope nor confidence, but only constant fear."

Martin Luther's exhortations to the Knights were endless, and his words were chipping away at their armor more than the slings and arrows of the Prussians, Lithuanians, and Poles ever could. In the eyes of the Catholic Church, he was nothing short of a satanic tempter to damnation. The Vatican saw Luther as its arch-nemesis, a Protestant Darth Vader entreating the Teutonic Knights to leave the Holy Mother Church and come to join him on the dark side.

To be fair, tensions between the peoples of Northern Europe and Southern Europe in regard to Roman Catholic control of religion had been brewing for a while. Even as the Teutonic Knights were attempting to stamp out the last vestiges of paganism in the hinterlands of northeastern Europe, many already Christianized Northern Europeans chafed under papal rule.

The Catholic Church had brought with it the ethos and many of the old traditions of the Roman Empire, and much of this was completely alien to Northern Europe. Thus the roots of Catholicism in Northern Europe were not quite as deep as they were in Italy, Spain, and even France. So it was relatively easy for someone like Martin Luther to come along and uproot the half-formed ideology that the Vatican's emissaries had planted.

Even so, no one imagined the Teutonic Knights would follow suit. But by getting to know the Grand Master of the Order on a personal basis, Luther discovered his pressure points and figured out just how to split him from the Catholic faith. He understood that Albert was fed up with being just another lapdog of the Pope; the leader of the Teutonic Knights craved temporal power of his own. He found it when he left the Church and the Order behind to become the first Duke of Prussia.

It was an incredible transformation that made the Duchy of Prussia essentially the very first Protestant state. Just as the Catholic Church had won the Roman Empire with the conversion of Constantine—or more recently the Grand Duchy of Lithuania with Jogaila's conversion—Luther had turned an entire nation into a Protestant stronghold by turning its leader.

He did not turn most of the Teutonic Knights, however; although some left with Albert, most remained loyal to the Roman Catholic Church. The Holy Roman Emperor appointed a new Grand Master named Walther of Cronberg, and life went on in the Order's few remaining territories on the outskirts of the Holy Roman Empire and Livonia. It had been a long road from paganism to Protestantism, and the original mission of the Teutonic Knights had gotten lost somewhere along the way, but for the next few decades, Livonia at least would remain a potent regional force.

The Shadow Wars

In the year 1547, in the Russian lands to the east of the Teutonic domain of Livonia, a new king was crowned. This monarch began his rule with the rather bland name of Ivan IV, but he would end his reign of terror with the well-earned title of Ivan the Terrible. He was the first Russian monarch to truly weaponize fear in order to keep both his friends and his enemies in check. He was a ruthless captain of the ship of state who managed to tame the Tatars and even intimidate the Mongols.

And once he had the eastern half of his empire under control, it wasn't long before he began testing the resolve of Livonia and the Teutonic Knights situated near Russia's western frontier. It was the year 1558 when Ivan the Terrible sent his soldiers to Livonia in the hope of subjugating the territory and gaining a strategic port on the Baltic Sea.

At first, the overwhelming numbers of Ivan's men seemed destined for an easy victory over this Teutonic holdout. They quickly gained a strong foothold in the territory of eastern Livonia, where they also had local sentiment on their side: Many Livonians hated their Teutonic overlords. But when Sweden, Poland, and Denmark all decided to intervene on the side of the Knights, it was Ivan the Terrible who had reason to be concerned. The Russian war machine came to a grinding halt in the town of Revel, and the bloody stalemate that ensued lasted until the summer of 1560—when the Battle of Ermes resulted in complete disaster for the Teutons.

The main branch of the Livonian Teutonic Knights, led by Marshal Philipp Schall von Bell, was stationed on the front lines in what today constitutes the nation of Latvia. Their trouble began when they spotted a small group of Russian horsemen on the outskirts of their territory. Believing they could easily overpower the Russians, the Knights charged directly at them. But it turned out that this contingent was a scouting party for a massive Russian army positioned close behind. The pursuing Knights soon became the pursued, and they were quickly outflanked and surrounded. The Russians now had every opportunity to live up to their Tsar's terrible title. Some 12,000 of them made short work of the thousand or so Teutonic Knights caught in their trap. Hacking limbs and chopping off heads, the Russian soldiers killed nearly 300 of the Knights and forced the rest to surrender.

Even after this brutal defeat, the struggle continued, and after many deaths on both sides, the Russians were finally expelled from Livonia in 1578. But by then the Teutonic Knights had agreed to relinquish control of the territory to Poland, leaving them with only a few scattered holdings inside the Holy Roman Empire. Without a state of their own, the Order became basically an auxiliary military force in the service of the Holy Roman Empire and the Habsburgs, a commitment that would last until the 1918 dissolution of the Austro-Hungarian Empire following World War One.

In the intervening centuries, the Order played walk-on roles in several conflicts, most famously in 1683, when an army of Ottoman Turks was at the gates of Vienna and a battalion of Teutonic Knights was among the reinforcements that arrived just in time to drive them off. Their last major battle came a little over a decade later, in 1697, when the Ottomans attempted to invade Hungary and the Teutonic Knights arrived on the scene to help ensure a Christian victory in the Battle of Zenta. The Turks were sorely defeated in this clash, and the once mighty power of the Ottoman Empire would be on the defensive for the rest of its existence.

Throughout the 18th century, the Teutonic Knights periodically trained with the Knights Hospitaller on the island of Malta, but the days of regimented warfare were behind them. Their military character would last until the early 20th century, but members only served individually as officers in other armed forces. The Shadow Wars were long over, and there would be no more organized Teutonic armies arriving in the nick of time to save Europe from disaster.

The Teutonic Knights, Revolution, and the Third Reich

The Teutonic Order's slow decline sped up considerably during the French Revolution of the 1790s when it lost its holdings in Belgium and all territories west of the Rhine. It's no surprise that a monastic order of knights would be targeted by the revolution's atheist thinkers. After all, the radical left of Paris initially wanted to oust Christianity from the country completely. However, this was an incredibly unrealistic goal, since the rural majority of Frenchmen were devout Catholics who had no use for the intellectual madness being espoused by the likes of Maximilien Robespierre and his cronies.

General Napoleon Bonaparte realized this truth early on in his career, and in order to consolidate his power, he allied himself with the Vatican, promising to protect the faith. But once Napoleon became Emperor, it turned out that this protection did not extend to monastic military orders. In 1805, Napoleon officially dissolved everything that remained of the Teutonic Order within his hastily acquired empire. This deprived the Knights of most of their territory east of the Rhine as well, significantly diminishing their already much-reduced geographical footprint and leaving them with only what remained in the Holy Roman Empire.

Even after Napoleon's eventual defeat, requests for a return of Teutonic property fell on deaf ears. As the former French Emperor languished in exile on Saint Helena, the mistrustful Knights languished in Austria, essentially going underground for the next few decades in fear of further attack. They only resurfaced in 1839 after the Austrian Emperor Ferdinand I reassured them that they did indeed have a place in his Empire and reformed the group as a modern charitable organization. Instead of marching into battle themselves, they would now operate military hospitals to care for injured troops on the front lines of Austria's many wars.

In 1871, Pope Pius IX re-consecrated what remained of the Catholic branch of the Order, giving them new rules and discipline. This new charter continued all the way through World

War One. The Great War—as it was known at the time—started in 1914 when a Serbian nationalist named Gavrilo Princip assassinated Austria's Archduke, Franz Ferdinand. In that same year, the Teutonic Knights managed to enlist over 1,500 charitable sponsors from the Austrian aristocracy and provide care for as many as 3,000 injured soldiers. The Austro-Hungarian Empire ultimately lost the war, however, and the Knights lost their last little place on the world stage. Relegated to utter obscurity, they barely eked out an existence with what remained of their support in Austria.

And then, during the darkest part of Germanic—and no doubt world—history, the Teutonic Knights found themselves in an altogether schizophrenic and almost intolerable position. All throughout Adolf Hitler's rise to power, the Nazis had placed the Teutonic Knights of old on a pedestal as exemplars of German martial virtue and former glory. But it must be stressed that this fascist hero worship was not something that the Knights themselves had ever invited—and furthermore that at the very same time this exaltation of everything Teutonic was taking place, the Nazi Party was actively persecuting the living, breathing members of the Teutonic Order! This was indeed a very strange time to be a Teutonic Knight.

During the late 1930s the Nazis, under Hitler's direction, systematically shut down every Teutonic bastion they encountered. It was an especially ironic example of the fascist penchant for eliminating any and every organization rooted outside of state control. Before the Anschluss, you could see Teutonic Knights taking part in state parades and charitable functions throughout Austria, and they were a well-established part of civic culture and community events in Vienna. When the Nazis came to town, all such festivities were promptly canceled.

Yet even as the Gestapo was busy rounding up members of the Teutonic Order and confiscating their property, they were hijacking their history and attempting to warp it to their own ends. It was Heinrich Himmler, Hitler's henchman for everything mystical and esoteric, who sought to mold the soldiers of the SS into a new Teutonic Order. This required a series of ideological somersaults on Himmler's part since while he loved the legacy of the fighting order of Teutonic Knights, he deeply despised anything to do with the Catholic Church.

He attempted to reconcile these contradictory views by suggesting that the "spirit" of the Teutonic Knights had existed long before their association with Catholicism. Himmler sought to trace the Knights' origin to the pre-Christian Germanic tribes who had struggled against the Roman Empire and also linked them to the Vikings. Serious historians find the theory ridiculous since, in reality, the Vikings were the very kind of pagans the Teutonic Order was tasked with stamping out.

However, Himmler wasn't the only one to question the truth about what the Teutonic Knights actually were, and what they represented. These very questions were the focus of a little-known book called *The Thousand Year Conspiracy* was written by Paul Winkler in 1943. The book is classified as nonfiction, and the author insists that what he has to say is true, but there is no solid evidence for its main claims. Basically, Winkler asserts that the Teutonic Knights were never really Christian, to begin with. They feigned Christianity on the surface, but in reality, they held fast to the old Germanic religion and ideals from the pre-Christian past. Winkler then goes on to allege that the Knights have ties to various cult-like Germanic groups.

It may seem absurd to claim that a Christian order dedicated to stamping out pagans in Eastern Europe was in fact secretly pagan itself, but Winkler makes his case with a completely straight face. He also contends that Himmler had unearthed documents that verifying the theory. And it must be admitted that—whether or not he actually found any such thing—Himmler was certainly trying his best. To aid him in this effort, he even created a special group of archeologists, anthropologists, linguists, and mystics—the Ahnenerbe—and sent them to scour the globe for links to Germany's Teutonic past.

This strange group and their efforts were partially immortalized in the Steven Spielberg blockbuster *Raiders of the Lost Ark*, which has intrepid archaeologist Indiana Jones keeping a wary eye on a group of Nazis searching for the lost Ark of the Covenant. Spielberg certainly had a great plot on his hands with this one. The only thing is, it wasn't entirely fiction. The Ahnenerbe really *were* looking for the Ark, just as they were looking for the Holy Grail and the so-called "Spear of Destiny". What was the Spear of Destiny, you might ask? Well, according to legend, it was nothing short of the spear that pierced the side of Christ on the Cross.

As the biblical account goes, a Roman soldier stabbed Jesus with his spear and released a fountain of blood and water. What you won't find in the gospels is that this also released a mystical power that imbued the spear with a supernatural force such that, from that day forward, whosoever possessed it held the fate of the entire world in his hands. According to this legend, the spear gave its wielder the ability to forge empires and bring nations under his control. And some say that it was over this relic that the Teutonic Order was forged. You see, the Spear of Destiny apparently has a pesky habit of disappearing from world history and then reappearing at opportune times. In this account, it was lost shortly after the fall of Rome but subsequently rediscovered in the Middle Ages, leading to the formation of the Teutonic Knights.

At any rate, while all of this propagandized wrangling of history, myths, and legends was taking place in regard to the Teutonic past, those few souls still under the banner of the Teutonic Knights were being more sorely persecuted than at any other time in their history. The Nazis deemed them a secret society and viewed them with the same suspicion as Freemasons, Communists, and Jehovah's Witnesses. They wanted nothing more than to shut the Teutonic Knights down for good, and in 1939 they officially made the Order illegal and seized all of its land holdings—continuing all the while to use its legacy for their own ends.

As it happened, this played right into the hands of the Nazis' soon-to-be adversaries in the Soviet Union. It was the invading Teutonic Knights, after all, whom the Russians had so spectacularly defeated during the Battle of the Ice back in 1242. And so, in rousing 20th-century Russians to stand up to the German threat, it was only natural for the Soviet propagandists to paint the Nazis with the same Teutonic brush with which they were busily painting themselves.

In the years leading up to World War Two, speeches were given and articles were written reminding patriotic Soviets to stand strong in the face of Teutonic aggression. Acclaimed filmmaker Sergei Eisenstein, the Spielberg of the Soviet Union, even got into the act with his 1938 historical epic *Alexander Nevsky*, which includes a dramatic depiction of the moment of the Russian victory over the Teutons in the Battle of the Ice. Ironically, Joseph Stalin ended up banning this brilliant propaganda piece when German-Soviet relations seemed to have improved after the signing of the infamous Molotov–Ribbentrop Pact.

But as any student of history knows, it wasn't long before this nonaggression pact unraveled, Germany invaded, and the Russians once again demonized their adversaries as the same evil Teutonic Knights they had battled on the ice all those years ago. As always, history has an incredible way of repeating itself.

Going Full Circle

It is estimated that no more than a dozen Teutonic Knights were still officially active at the end of World War Two. It was a spectacular decline for a group that had once numbered in the tens of thousands. And those who remained—although no longer raising sword and shield to fend off enemies—had an uphill battle in their struggle to keep the Order alive through the postwar decades. After being tossed around like an ideological football in the Second World War, they faced even more degradation during the Cold War, especially within the Communist Bloc. When the Iron Curtain came crashing down on Eastern Europe, it cut them off even further from their glory days, and most of their property was once again seized—this time by the Communists.

In many ways, the Teutonic Knights are still attempting to recover. They have since regained land holdings in both Austria and Slovenia, but they are certainly a far cry from the days of the Monastic State. The Knights haven't given up, however, and it was only recently that they petitioned the government of the Czech Republic to return the famed Bouzov Castle and the surrounding land.

The modern-day Order consists of around one thousand members, mostly priests, and nuns whose primary focus is faith, charity, and caring for the sick. It seems that the Teutonic Knights have truly gone full circle, back to the roots that were planted long ago among the sick and dying at that makeshift German hospital in the Holy Land.

Further Reading and Reference

This appendix presents some of the reading and reference material that made this book possible. If you would like to dig deeper into the history of the Teutonic Knights, the following sources are an excellent place to start.

The Thousand Year Conspiracy: Secret Germany Behind the Mask. Paul Winkler

If you consider yourself a conspiracy buff, you are going to love this one! Written at the height of World War Two and seemingly lost in the shuffle of other war titles being pumped out during that time, it was only recently rediscovered. Now, some 75 years after the fact, Winkler's startling claims are finally being examined in detail.

As Winkler tells it, the Germanic tribes, the Holy Roman Empire, the Kingdom of Prussia, and the Third Reich were all part and parcel of the same Germanic imperial ambition—and the Teutonic Knights were studious caretakers of that ambition throughout all of these transformations. According to Winkler, the German lust for Lebensraum has never gone away; it has just adeptly changed names and titles throughout the ages. It must be stressed that Winkler's ideas haven't been proven, but they are quite fascinating nonetheless.

The Ottoman Empire: 1326–1699. Stephen Turnbull

Of course, you cannot talk about a Crusader order such as the Teutonic Knights without mentioning the mighty Muslim Empire that all surviving Crusader orders eventually fought against—the Ottoman Empire. This book by Stephen Turnbull is entertaining, fascinating, and never once deviates from the facts. It takes you down a strict timeline, following the twists and turns of each battle as it unfolded. This text serves as an excellent reference with regard to some of the Teutonic Knights' later battles.

A History of the Popes. Joseph McCabe
Since the popes were the ultimate superiors of the Teutonic Order, it is important to have a basic understanding of the Vatican and the papacy if you want to really understand the Knights. As the title just might imply, this book is a complete history of the popes from the ancient era to the present day. It gives you a thorough rundown of all the popes, discussing at length every aspect of their reigns from the high points to the low. This book has just about everything that you need to know about the papacy.

The Clash of Cultures on the Medieval Baltic Frontier. Alan V. Murray
It truly was a clash of cultures when the Central European Teutonic Knights stormed into the Eastern European frontier of the Baltic. As these cross-bearing Christian knights waged war against their tree-worshiping pagan contemporaries, the contrast between the opposing sides was just as striking as in the initial Crusades launched against the Holy Land itself. This book not only provides important details about the war in the Knights waged in the Baltic, it also gives great insight as to the many personal motivations behind the struggle.

The History of the Lithuanian Nation: And its Present National Aspirations. Kunigas Antanas Jusaitis
This is an old book, written in the early 20th century, but it still holds invaluable information regarding the rise of Lithuania. The book is also surprisingly entertaining, with the author providing much humor along with his many insights into the long road of Lithuanian history. The pages of this book may be yellow with age, but it is still very much relevant to this very day.

The History of Poland: From the Earliest Times to the Present Day. Major F. E. Whitton

This book is another one from the turn of the 20th century, and it gives great insight into the history of another nation heavily involved in Teutonic history—Poland. For our purposes, it probably provides a bit of an overload of data on the general history of Poland, and it is much scanter when it comes to the doings of the Teutonic Knights themselves. Nevertheless, there are some real jewels of information that can be found in this book.

The Holy Blood and the Holy Grail. Michael Baigent, Richard Leigh

This book has been making the rounds for a while now, and it's mostly about the Knights Templar. Dan Brown is said to have based much of his bestselling novel *The Da Vinci Code* on what he read in this very book. However, it also mentions some rather interesting facts about the Teutonic Knights. If you are interested in learning more, I encourage you to check it out.

Crusader Castles of the Teutonic Knights: The red-brick castles of Prussia 1230–1466. Stephen Turnbull

Although the main emphasis here is on the many castles and fortresses that the Teutonic Knights built all across Eastern Europe, this book also holds some very interesting and often surprising commentary on the Teutonic Knights themselves. You get some rare glimpses of what monastic life was really like— even how the Knights would attach tall towers to the sides of their castles to serve as bathrooms so that human excrement could be dumped from the top into latrines below. In his research on the Teutonic Knights Stephen Turnbull is quite meticulous, and you just never know what you might learn!

The Teutonic Knights: A Military History. **William Urban**

This piece by Professor William Urban is probably going to be your most helpful resource when it comes to chronicling the main events of Teutonic history. Here you can find all the details about how individual battles went down. Urban is a lifelong scholar of everything to do with the Crusades, and his work truly is worth checking out.

The Spear of Destiny. **Trevor Ravenscroft**

This page-turner delves into some fascinating conspiracy theories in regard to the Spear of Destiny. Trevor examines the world's fascination with this alleged relic, and in particular, the obsession shared by Hitler and Himmler. Along with this main narrative, the book does indeed intersect with the tale of the Teutonic Knights. If you are interested in supernatural lore, legends, and conspiracy theories, this book might be of interest to you.

Also by Conrad Bauer

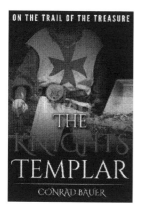 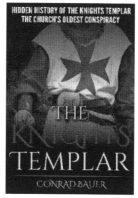 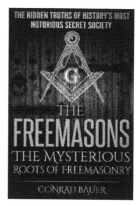

 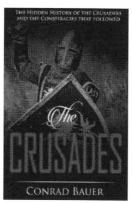 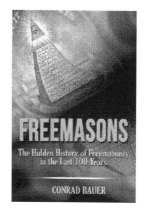

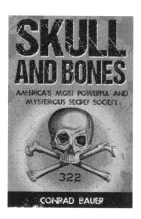  

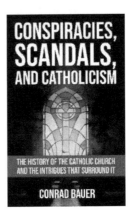

Made in United States
Orlando, FL
01 June 2023